# SPONTI-SPRÜCHE · ENGLISCH

Gesammelt von Fred Meyer-Wefel

## SAVE WATER, BATH WITH A FRIEND



Eichborn

# We are happily divorced.

Die Fotos stammen aus dem Bildband »City Indians«, in England fotografiert von Chris Wróblewski, 1983 bei uns im Eichborn Verlag erschienen.

CIP-Kurztitelaufnahme der Deutschen Bibliothek
*Sponti-Sprüche englisch:* save water, bath with
a friend / Fred Meyer-Wefel (Hrsg.). —
Frankfurt am Main: Eichborn, 1985.
ISBN 3-8218-1939-1
NE: Meyer-Wefel, Fred [Hrsg.]

 · Cover: Uwe Gruhle unter Verwendung eines dpa-Fotos · Gesamtherstellung: Fuldaer Verlagsanstalt GmbH · ISBN 3-8218-1939-1 · Verlagsverzeichnis schickt gern: Eichborn Verlag, D-6000 Frankfurt 70.

# Vorwort

Wenn einem der Boden unter den Füßen weggezogen wird — und wann wird er das nicht —, muß man immer noch nicht auf den Mund fallen. Erst wenn man nichts mehr zur Antwort geben kann, ist man völlig dem Gesetz des freien Falls ausgeliefert. Die Spucke bleibt einem weg, bis sich das treffende, das erlösende Wort auf die Zunge gelegt hat. Und je leichter ich mich mit jenem Wort nehme, desto weniger schmerzhaft der Aufprall. (Das ist für die, die in der Schule nicht aufgepaßt haben, die zentrale, unverfälschte Aussage des Newtonschen Gesetzes.)
Die Fähigkeit, sprachlich auch auf die schwierigsten, die unmöglichsten Situationen reagieren zu können, diese Fähigkeit, mit dem Wort das Mißgeschick zu bannen und dem Zwang von Situation und Konvention seine Gewalt zu nehmen, halte ich für eine große englische Tugend. Der richtige Spruch im rechten Augenblick, der Spruch, mit dem man den anderen den Wind aus den Segeln nimmt — und diese anderen, dazu rechnen nicht nur die anderen, eben du und du und du und manchmal ich selbst, sondern auch die Lehrer, die Politiker, die großen Werte, die Werbung, Mama und Papa, die Vernunft, der gute Geschmack, die Weisheit, der Lebenssinn, das gan-

ze System. Was bleibt ist Punk und Limerick. Darum ist die englische Kultur die geistige Heimat, sorry, das Planschbecken aller Spontis!
Man lese nur einmal bei Newtons Landsmann und Kollegen Oscar Wilde nach. Da finden sich brillante Studien zum freien Fall auf dem Parkettboden. Z. B. in dem Theaterstück »An Ideal Husband«: lobt doch dort ein Lord einen Politiker, um gleichzeitig seinen eigenen, ebenfalls anwesenden Sohn fertig zu machen: »You have got what we want so much in political life nowadays — high character, high moral tone, high principles. (zu seinem Sohn): Everything that you have not got, sir, and never will have.« Worauf der Sohn antwortet: »I don't like principles, father. I prefer prejudices.«
Oscar war ein ächter Sponti, believe it or not. Wie sehr hätte er den technischen Fortschritt begrüßt: all die großen Betonflächen und die so praktischen Spraydosen. Dieser Fortschritt ist mir auch zugute gekommen, denn Graffiti gibt's umsonst. Von denen habe ich mir eine ganze Reihe für das Buch hier gemerkt. Andere Sprüche stammen aus dem Volksmund. Da habe ich allen meinen englischen Freunden zu danken, die für mich gesammelt und mich mit Spruchweisheiten unterhalten haben, besonders denke ich, Charles, an die gemeinsamen netten Abende im Buckingham Palace. Eine dritte, sehr kleine Gruppe bilden Zitate. Dabei ist mir ein Spruch

von Mae West dazwischen geraten, das ist natürlich nicht die feine englische Art.
Viele gute Sprüche mußte ich fortlassen, weil sie zu sehr vom englischen Sprachwitz bestimmt waren, und den versteht halt hier nicht jeder Sponti, und Berlitz hilft auch nicht immer. Dafür habe ich aber ein paar Sprüche, die mir aus dem Deutschen bekannt waren, ins Englische übertragen. Welche verrat' ich nicht, weil ich gerne wissen möchte, ob das einer merkt, vor allem einer meiner englischen Freunde. Die glauben nämlich immer noch, daß wir auf dem Kontinent nichts gelernt haben. Aber wir haben jetzt die Sponti-Sprüche! Schön wäre übrigens, wenn sich das Wort »Sponti-Sprüche«, wie schon das Wort »Kindergarten«, im Englischen einbürgern würde. Es könnte doch der Völkerverständigung dienen.
Zum Schluß möchte ich noch meiner Freundin Claire für ihre Arbeitsunterstützung danken.

*Fred Meyer-Wefel*

**A definition of pornography
— reading material
to be held in one hand.**

**A giraffe is
the highest form of life.**

**A pessimist is
an optimist with experience.**

**A sure sign
that your marriage is at an end
— when all that is stiff
is his socks.**

**A woman
who would prefer to be a man
is rather unambitious.**

Adam came before Eve
. . . and then he
helped her come.

**All men were equal before God. After him there are differences.**

Always wear a watch —
you will know where to stop
when you wash your hands.

Archduke Franz Ferdinand
has been found
alive and well and living
in Sussex.
First World War was a mistake.

**According to statistics
the main cause of divorce
is marriage.**

**As long as
we are free to dream
we dream of freedom.**

**At least masturbation
is sex with
someone you love.**

**At first I thought
he was the world to me
— but since then
I've done some geography.**

# Back to Nature — but not on foot.

**Be a good neighbour — don't listen to conversations through the wall.**

**Be realistic — stand nearer.**
(Im Herrenklo)

**Before you find your prince you have to kiss a hell of a lot of frogs.**

**Better a hair in the soup than the soup in your hair.**

**Beat inflation — rob a bank.**

**Better behind than not at all.**

**Buy an atlas and see the world.**

**Can you tell the age of an onion by counting its rings?**

**Crawlers never stumble.**

**Coming soon to bookshops everywhere — this wall in a paperback edition.**

(Wand eines Londoner Buchladens.)

# Come to Lapland for your honeymoon. The nights last twenty-four hours.

**Death is nature's way of giving you a rest.**

# Democracy is too good for the masses.

Did you hear about the woman
who killed her husband
with a bow and arrow?
She didn't want to wake the children.

**Discuss the view that writing graffiti is the purest form of art because it is done neither for financial reward nor for personal glory.**

Does it hurt? —
Only when I laugh.

**Don't adjust your mind, there's a fault in reality.**

**Don't be wasteful. Use both sides ot the paper.**

(Toilette in Leeds.)

**Don't bother repenting. The world has already ended.**

(Graffiti an einer Kirchentür in Birmingham.)

**Don't call for help at night — you might wake the neighbours.**

**Don't drink and drive — its rather difficult to turn the steering wheel.**

# Don't go to work — there's a lot to do.

**Don't panic.**
**Count to ten —**
**then panic.**

**Don't shout at me.**
**I'm not a traffic warden.**

**Don't throw peanuts.**
**Show some respect**
**for your ancestors.**
(Graffiti in einem Zoo.)

**Do unto others**
**as you would have them do unto you.**
**— I can't.**
**I'm a masochist.**

**Don't vote, the government will get in.**

**Don't walk on the grass. Smoke it.**

**Double your income — photocopy your pay cheques.**

**Drinking won't solve your problems, but it will give you lots of interesting new ones.**

Dying isn't so bad,
but you feel bloody awful
the next day.

Eat cow dung.
Ten billion flies can't be wrong.

# Electrician seeks contacts.

Even dwarves started small.

# Even your inferiority complex is better than mine.

**Every exaggeration gets nearer the truth.**

**Everyone is of some use — they can always be a bad example.**

**Everyone should live within his means these days — even if he has to borrow to do it.**

**Everyone's always complaining about the weather. But nobody is doing anything about it.**

Everything is fine with the world —
one mile under ground.

Everything is going to the dogs — including, fortunately, morals.

Everything that's any fun
is either immoral,
illegal or fattening.

Examinations — Nature's answer to constipation.

**Feel superior,**
**fondle a nun.**

# Fight low pay — work harder.

**First of all you learn**
**to speak and walk**
**— later you're told**
**to sit still and keep**
**your mouth shut.**

**For everyday feminine protection**
**— try a machine gun.**

**Fucking you is so boring
I have to count sheep
to keep awake.**

**Get married
and share the problems
you didn't know you had.**

**Get rid of sexual tension,
make an obscene phone call.**

**Girls, make sure
you have beauty rather than brains.
Men can see better
than they can think!**

**Go to church on Sunday
and avoid the Christmas rush.**

**Go gay and save on contraceptives.**

**Go on holiday this winter ... and save money on deckchair hire.**

**Gone for lunch.
Back in half an hour.
Godot.**

**God isn't dead — just very ill.**

**Gone for breakfast.
If I'm not here by 12.30.,
gone for lunch as well.**

(Nachricht an einer Ladentür in London.)

Having an erection is
like a mathematical problem —
the longer you think about it,
the harder it gets.

He who isn't feeling confused
must have been misinformed.

He who laughs last
has only just got the joke.

**Healthy people live longer — but they spend more time jogging.**

**Help the police —**
**beat yourself up!**

# Help to support wild life — have an orgy.

**His conscience is clean**
**— he's never used it!**

# Hot dogs don't bite.

**How does a girl get a mink?**
**The way a mink gets a mink.**

**How is your seafood diet going?**
**— It's great.**
**I see food and I eat it.**

# Hypochondria is the only disease I haven't got . . .

**I am the type of kid
my mother told me
not to play with.**

**I am very interested in graffiti
— served with a bolognese sauce.**

# I can resist anything - except temptation.

I couldn't get on
with contact lenses.
My glasses got in the way.

I don't expect the worst.
I can't wait for it!

# I don't know what I want but I know how to get it.

I just saw God . . .
and she was black.

I first met my wife here.
— So did I.
Isn't she great!

(Im Wartesaal eines Standesamts in Bristol.)

**I go to sleep early at night and get up late in the morning — but I lie awake for hours in the afternoon.**

**I guarantee your satisfaction or double your rubbish back. The dustman.**

**I have two daughters — both girls.**

**I hope we grow as old as we look.**

**I may be illiterate
but I'm good at graffiti.**

**I only drink on my own
or in company.**

**I pursued knowledge
— but it was
too fast for me.**

# I used to be really sceptical of Christianity until I realized I was God.

**If sex is a pain in the arse
— try doing it another way.**

# If they are right about evolution, why have we only got one pair of hands?

## If you are confused, you are misinformed!

(Graffiti, Cambridge University.)

## If you don't believe in luck, how else can you explain your enemies' success?

(In einer Halle für Glücksspiele in London.)

## If you stick your head in the sand today you'll be grinding your teeth tomorrow.

**If you throw your old cigarettes in the toilet, how am I supposed to light them?**

**I'm all for womens movements — as long as they are regular!**

**I'm leaving home . . . as soon as we get one.**

**I'm not bald — I just have a rather wide parting.**

**In case of fire do not use lift — just jump!**

(In einem Fahrstuhl in Leicester.)

Incest — a game for the whole family.

Is dying hereditary?

Is that a gun in your pocket or are you just pleased to see me?
Mae West

In case your luggage label gets lost — write on both sides.

It begins when you sink
into his arms;
and it ends with
your arms in his sink.

It's becoming
more and more difficult
to live simply.

**It's best to be
at the centre of things
— then you get in
everybody's way.**

It's best to tell the truth
— then nobody believes you.

It's great to have a job
— pity about the work.

It's lonely in the saddle
since the horse died.

It's not enough simply to bath — you must change the water occasionally.

It's not enough to have no opinion. You must also be unable to express it.

It's really cool to be dead.

I've often asked myself what kind of idiot writes on walls, and now I know.

(Graffiti in Brackley.)

**I tried using a toilet brush**
**but now I've gone back**
**to using paper.**

**I trust in God alone.**
**All others pay cash.**

**I used to be indecisive,**
**but now I'm not so sure.**
**Boscoe Pertwee.**

**I want to find a husband!**
**Wouldn't a single man**
**be a better idea?**

**If Columbus hadn't discovered**
**America we'd have been**
**spared a lot.**

Is there life after marriage?

# I'm telling you for the hundred-thousandth time, stop exaggerating!

It's so expensive
to have children these days
that only the poor
seem to be able
to afford them.

In life the first fifty years
are the text
— the rest is the commentary.

**Jesus saves . . .
and with inflation,
that's a miracle.**

**Join the army,
travel the world,
meet interesting
people — and kill
them!**

**Join the campaign
to make graffiti writing illegal.**

(Graffiti in Oxford.)

# Keep London tidy — eat a tourist.

# Keep our country green — fuck a frog.

# Keep your ears open — but your legs crossed.

# Life is too short for long faces.

## Lavatory attendants of the world unite — you have nothing to lose but your chains.

## Living is bad for your health.

## Living takes up a lot of our time.

# Make love during the safe period — when his wife's away.

**Make love not war.
I'm married
I do both.**

**Make money in your spare time
— blackmail your friends.**

**Marriage is
the chief cause of divorce.**

**Make love not war —**
**see me for details.**

**Make analysis more anal.**

**Marx is dead,**
**Lenin is dead**
**and I'm not feeling**
**too good either.**

**Money doesn't bring happiness**
**— but it makes unhappiness**
**easier to put up with.**

**Money isn't everything . . .**
**but it's not bad for a start.**

**My cold is better this morning**
**— I've been practising all night.**

Making love is
like having a bank account.
After you withdraw
you lose interest.

Marriage is the best way
of finding out
what sort of man your wife
would have really preferred.

## Masturbation is better — you don't have to give your hand flowers beforehand and apologize afterwards.

Modesty is the art
of letting others find out
how important you are.

**Mother held her little daughter / fifteen minutes under water, / not to give her any trouble / but to see the water bubble.**

Mummy, Daddy just fell
of the roof.
I know. He waved
as he went past.

Masochists tell all under torture
— out of gratitude.

# My favourite dance is decadance.

My husband left me
for my best friend
— and I really miss her.

# No Easter this year — they found the body.

Nobody loves me —
why should I?

# O.K., so your boy-friend has hairs on his chest — but then so has Lassie.

**Oral sex is a matter of taste.**

# Our lips met passionately — then she closed her legs and broke my glasses.

**Parking for regular customers only.**

(Auf einem Parkschild vor einem Londoner Beerdigungsinstitut.)

# People who work are too lazy to think.

**People who write graffiti on walls are only following God's example.**

**Prevent accidents on the roads — drive on the pavement.**

**Prevent hangovers. Stay drunk!**

# Please don't throw cigarette ends on the floor — the cock-roaches are getting lung cancer.

**Pull the flush before you rise.
And you will get
a nice surprise.**

(Klospruch in Northampton.)

**Quick, get me a hammer!
There's a fly in my soup.**

Reality is for people
who can't cope with drugs.

**Revenge is sweet
— and calorie-free!**

Robinson Crusoe
was the only person
who got all his work
done by Friday.

Ronald Reagan
is good for nothing . . .
and that's his strong point.

Rugbyplayers suffer
from breast envy.

Seven hours of school is better than no sleep at all.

Sex appeal — please give generously.

**Sex is bad for you — but good for us.**

Sex is quite enjoyable but it's nothing compared to the real thing.

Sterility is hereditary!

Sado-masochism means
not having to say
you are sorry.

San Francisco is the only city
where a working-class man
can live like a queen.

Save water —
bath with a friend.

Stop the world
I want to get off.

Stop repeating
yourself. Try
something original
— like suicide.

Sex in the desert is better
than sand in bed.

Suicide is the most
sincere form of self-criticism.

Support Women's Liberation
— make him sleep
on the wet patch.

Standards are higher now
— but no one can
live up to them.

**Stop vandalism —
or we'll smash your
window!**

Stop your rice from sticking together
— boil each grain separately.

(Graffiti in einem chinesischen Kochbuch.)

**Take up belly-dancing — the only job where you start in the middle.**

**Tell the orgasm I'm coming.**

# The best things that life has to offer are duty free.

**The best three things in life are a drink before and a cigarette afterwards.**

**The driver of this van is Indian — smoke signals only.**

# The first three minutes of life are the most dangerous — except for the last three minutes.

**The flesh was willing but the grass was wet.**

**The great thing about life is that it's only temporary.**

**The height of laziness — holding a cocktail shaker and waiting for an earthquake.**

**The Jews are God's chosen people. The Eskimos are God's frozen people.**

**The only people who come regularly are postmen.**

The advantage of masturbation
is that you don't have
to look your best.

The best means
of crime prevention
is to abolish the police.

The future has been cancelled
owing to lack of interest.

The important thing is
that we are moving forwards —
never mind the direction.

The more you forget yourself,
the better others will
remember later.

The one who survives a tragedy
is not it's hero.

The sooner you die
the longer you're dead.

The trouble with bigamy is
having two mothers-in-law.

The trouble with political humor is
that so many jokes get elected.

The trouble with self-made men is
that they worship their creator.

The trouble with this driver is
he keeps trying to overtake.
(Graffiti in einer Straßenbahn.)

**There are more old alcoholics than old doctors.**

# The only problem with doing nothing is that you never know when you've finished.

**The only problem with the younger generation is that I don't belong to it any more.**

**The only thing my wife and I have in common is that we were married on the same day.**

**The only things which get screwed around here are the light bulbs.**

**The only women who aren't Les-
bians
are those who suppress it.**

# The problem with egoists is that they are more interested in themselves than in me.

**The only time
a fisherman tells the truth
is when he calls another
fisherman a liar.**

**The worst chewing gum
I have ever tasted.**

(Auf einem Automaten für Verhütungsmittel in Leeds.)

**The world will end tomorrow —
Come and join our protest
demonstration next Saturday.**

**There are two types of people —
those who make generalizations
and those, like me, who don't.**

**There is a meeting for
all the virgins in the school
to be held at 4 this afternoon
in the telephone box.**

**There may be no life on other
planets — but it's pretty difficult
on this one too.**

**There must be something wrong
with work if the rich give
it to the poor.**

Things were so different
before they all changed.

Think you've got problems?
My sun-dial is slow.

**Third World Aid means transferring money from the poor in rich countries to the rich in poor countries.**

This lavatory will be closed
for the rest of the week
because of industrial action
— so do what you can today.

To all virgins —
thanks for nothing.

To each his own —
to me the most!

Today is the beginning
of the rest of your life.

**Try meditating — its better than sitting on your ass all day.**

27% of men prefer
women with fat legs
and 15% prefer women with thin legs.
The other 58% prefer
something in between.

**Want to help save fuel supplies?
Be cremated with a friend.**

**Was Jesus the first pin up?**

**Why are you reading this, you idiot?
Watch what you're doing.**

(Nottingham, Herrenklo.)

**Why go to the cinema
to watch sex and violence
when you can see it at home?**

**We are happily divorced.**

# We are mere pimples on the arse of reality.

We are ready for anything
— but good for nothing.

We buy junk
and sell antiques.
(An einem Antiquitätengeschäft.)

# We drink to drown our sorrows but when we're drunk things seem to swim.

We have nothing to lose
but our fear.

We may be daft
but we're not bloody stupid.

**We want everything — and in large quantities.**

# We're always in the shit — only the depth varies.

**We've lost contact with reality — don't worry, it will find us again soon.**

**What has posterity done for me?**

**What is a lecture?
The way in which information is conveyed from the notes of the lecturer to the notes of the student without passing through the minds of either.**

**What can you give the woman who has everything?**
**Penicillin.**

**What is apathy?**
**I don't know and I don't care.**

# What is life but a sexually transmitted disease?

**What is not quite right today will be completely fucked up tomorrow.**

**What is the shortest bedtime story?**
**— No.**

**What we call work the Mexicans call siesta.**

**When a cannibal uses a knife and fork — is that progress?**

**When are the Americans going to try a sunlanding?**

**When God made man she was just experimenting.**

**When I feel a desire to work I sit quietly in a corner and wait until the feeling passes.**

**When in doubt make the right decision.**

**When in Rome do as the Romans do — pick a pocket.**

**Whenever I see his fingernails I'm glad I don't have to look at his feet.**

**Where do words go when you rub them out?**

# Who needs sex education when they can read graffiti?

**Whoever swims against the current has to swallow quite a lot.**

**Why is it that at the end of the money there is still so much of the month left over?**

# Without men the world would be full of happy, fat women.

**Why is virginity like a balloon? Because it only takes one prick to make it disappear.**

Why should the army
have all the fun?
Weapons for everyone!

Women like the simpler things
in life — like men.

Women may be the weaker sex
— but men are certainly
the weakest.

Working yourself to death
is the only socially acceptable
form of suicide.

## Would the last person to leave the country please switch off the lights.

**Would you describe yourself as indecisive?**
**— Well, yes and no.**

**Xerox your life**
**— if you lose it,**
**it's nice to have a copy.**

**Yesterday we were**
**on the edge of a precipice**
**— today we have taken**
**a big step forward.**

You are never alone
with schizophrenia.

**You don't have to be mad to survive — but it helps.**

You can do what you want here — whether you like it or not.

**You're only young once. After that you'll have to find another excuse.**

**You can't talk about unemployment
with all these people
killing time every day.**

# You have to go too far
# to see
# how far you can go.

**You could never give up
gambling now.
— I bet I could!**

Jede Menge Zoff / für Studienrat und Prof. Erste, einzige und ausführliche Anleitung zum Schummeln, Spicken und Vortäuschen von Prüfungswissen. Ein Buch, das jeden Notendurchschnitt sprunghaft verbessert. Listig, lustig, raffiniert. Schülerfreundlicher Preis: **10,— DM** (1024)

Das ist Schummeln total. Neue Tricks für Fortgeschrittene. Chemie, Taschenrechner, Homecomputer, Sender und Empfänger werden angewandt und wissenschaftliche Testverfahren übertölpelt. Dazu Mogelgeständnisse Prominenter. — Kaufen und ausprobieren! **10,— DM** (1033)

So werden Lehrer auf Trab gebracht! Jede Menge Tips, Hinweise, Handlungsanleitungen, Strategien und Gemeinheiten, wie man dumpfautoritäre Lehrkörper unter Streß setzt. **Das Lehrbuch für die effektive Schüler-Notwehr; nur 10,— DM** (1030)

Lehrer, Eltern, Chefs, Hauswirte ecetera denken, du bist blöd. Von wegen! Kohle von den Eltern, anständige Noten, geile Kleidung, Ausgang nach Lust und Laune — hol sie dir. Du hast massig Rechte. Welche? Nachschaun! Hier! **10,— DM** (1035)

An alle Bürger dieser Republik: Besorgt euch dieses Überlebensbuch gegen Bürokratenwillkür und Datenverarbeitung. Es liefert wirkungsvolle Tricks und Tips zum Ärgern der Beamtenseele. Das ist konstruktive Subversion, wie wir sie lieben. — Für alle, denen die verwaltete Welt stinkt. **10,— DM** (1019)

Lehrer, Kindergärtnerinnen, Hausbesitzer, Kontrolleure, Schrebergärtner und Kirchenvorsteher halten Kinder für halslose Ungeheuer. Ergo kriegen sie ihren Ratgeber zur Bekämpfung dieser Brut. Mit Kinderhasser-Lexikon im Anhang. — Auch für entnervte Eltern von Nutzen. Ätzende Zeichnungen. **10,— DM** (1816)

Die Kunst der Englisch-Verballhornung greift epidemisch um sich. Wir liefern das erste Buch zur neuen Seuche; mit den besten Gags und vielen Zeichnungen. — Los geht's: Laden Sie Ihre Freunde zur »Gockel-Schwanz«-Party (Cocktail) mit »super fire« (mords Brand) ein! **10,— DM** (1810)

This kitchen-english is strong Tabacco. Aus Tausenden von Einsendungen sind hier die besten Übersetzungs-Gags zusammengestellt. Tolle Zeichnungen und jede Menge Stoff zum Lachen — zu Hause und im Büro. **10,— DM** (1817)

Die irrsten Flops, die genialsten Versager — hier sind sie versammelt. Massenhaft Schadenfreude von der besten Sorte! — Der Westdeutsche Rundfunk urteilt so: »Seit das Lexikon der Niederlagen erschienen ist, kann das Guinness-Buch der Rekorde einpacken.« **16,80 DM** (1082)

Das Lexikon gegen Chefs und andere Ärgerlinge: denn Rache ist süß. Wir bieten massenhaft praktische Rezepte, wie man Bösewichtern ihre Gemeinheiten wirkungsvoll heimzahlt. Lesen und in Vorfreude schwelgen! **Viel Rache für nur 16,80 DM** (1087)

Die subversive Welle rollt. Jetzt geht's Bürokraten, Bonzen, Machtfetischisten, Ausbeutern, Computern, der Kulturmafia und anderen Wichtigtuern ans Leder. Das subversive Lexikon, pickepacke-voll mit erlebter, erprobter + erlogener Action, das deine Phantasie beflügelt. **16,80 DM** (1084)

Eine Sammlung, die es bisher nicht gab: derbe, aufmüpfige, listige, zweideutige, gescheite, erfrischende, aggressive und lustige Sprichwörter. — »Wenn die Zähne weg sind, hat die Zunge freies Spiel!« Stimmt doch. Oder? — Über 1200 schnodderige Sprichwörter. **16,80 DM** (1083)

Das Beste, was je in Scene-Sprache geschrieben wurde. 12 Grimmsche Märchen: Sterntaler auf'm Wahnsinnstrip, Frau Holle wedelt die Rheumadecken aus, eine Emanze erzählt Froschkönig etc. **Das ganze super (!) illustriert, 12,80 DM** (1811)

Der große Durchblick für alle Freaks, Spontis, Schlaffis, Softis, Flipper und Hänger sowie deren Verwandte und sonstige Fuzzis. Spitze — dieser Grundwortschatz für läppische **10,— DM** (1088)

Der alltägliche Wahnsinn treibt die Lachtränen aus den Augen, wenn Rauschenbach sich mit seinen Karikaturen drüber hermacht. Der Zeichner aus der Scene liefert hier sein Bestes. **Mit detailliertem Verhandlungsszenario zur Anbahnung des Beischlafs:** Trotzdem nur **10,— DM** (1809)

Bis die Alten was schnallen, ist so'n Teeny dem Zusammenbruch nahe. Echt! — Lustige Bildgeschichte hat an der Realität. Jeder Streich ein Volltreffer — und Zeichner Rauschenbach in Top-Form. Für **nur 10,— DM** hilfst Du dem Pappi auf's Fahrrad. (1812)

**Nichts klappt!** Bild ist quer statt hoch. Also dreh's rum!

Ein ... im Eichborn Verlag

Die Welt ist wüst — und die Wüste lebt. — Gerd Bauers gezeichnete »Berichte aus dem Jammertal« (1. Kapitel) sind schon genauso scharf wie »Die Triebe der Liebe« (8. Kapitel). — Die Presse: »Du hast'n Rad ab, Gerd. Aber echt geil gemacht, deine Bilder.« **10,— DM** (1815)

Der Haupt-Strip zieht dir die Schuhe aus: Aus dem Dorf abgezischt, macht Toni Karriere bei der NASA, landet auf'm Mars und darf dort steinige Äcker pflügen. Das ist echt out. — Rundrum jede Menge triebhafte Zeichnungen. Trotzdem nur **10,— DM** (1813)

Hier wird das komplette Alte Testament rasant runtererzählt. Mit Spaß und Spannung, »Sex and Crime«, für Christen und Nichtchristen. »Dieser unheilige Knüller« (Münchner Merkur) »fasziniert wie ein Gute-Nacht-Krimi« (Die Zeit). Der neue Weg zur alten Bibel, 848 heitere Seiten lang. **Nur 16,80 DM** (0100)

Endlich liegt es vor: das Handbuch zur Bestimmung der elbischen Wald-, Feld-, Wasser-, Haus-, Berg-, Hügel- und Luftgeister. 79 Bilder vom berühmten »Yellow-Submarine«-Zeichner Heinz Edelmann. Peter Rühmkorf: »Unentbehrlich für jeden Geisterseher und Gespensterkundler.« **320 Seiten dick, Leinen, 36,— DM** (1027)

Man sollte endlich fürs Nicht-Arbeiten bezahlt werden, weil es sowieso nicht genug Jobs gibt, meint John Hannah, der geniale Säufer und Schreiber (Transatlantik, Pflasterstrand). Du kreischst vor Lachen über Johns Lebensbeichte. Eine Delikatesse für Durchblicker. — Zieh's dir rein. **24,80 DM** (0123)

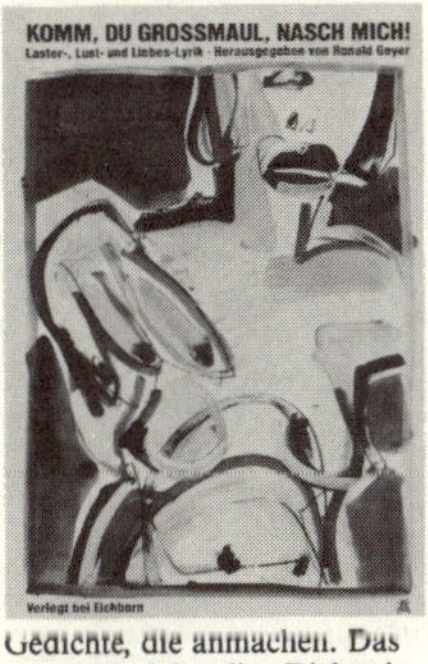


Gedichte, die anmachen. Das beste, was lebendige Dichterinnen und Dichter in den letzten Jahren zum Thema Nr. 1 geschrieben haben. Brutal und sensibel wie das Leben. Dabei sind: Theobaldy, Meyer, Karsunke, Fauser, Meckel, Nössler, Maiwald u. a. Mit Radierungen von Henry. **12,80 DM** (0311)

»Wenn sie mit dem Hintern wackelt, fließen die Flüsse bergauf«, schrieb Wolf Wondratschek. Jetzt gibt's den berühmten Bildband als Sonderheft für sage und schreibe **8,— DM** (7002)
Weiter in gut gebundener 7. Auflage lieferbar (die mit dem »Kodak-Foto-Buchpreis« ausgezeichnet wurde). Großformat. **28,— DM** (1701)

Die Buch-Sensation des Jahres! eine ausgebildete Soziologin tritt in der Peep-Show auf. Sie beschreibt aus ihrer Perspektive den Betrieb und ihre Kunden, die Männer. Vor allem aber: **sie fotografiert verdeckt.** Phantastisch geschrieben. Das ist wissenschaftliche Feldforschung! Das sind die Riten einer abgefuckten patriarchalischen Gesellschaft. **18,— DM** (1023)

Der verbogene Charakter im politischen Sumpf: karrieresüchtig, machtgeil, erfolgreich, servil und überheblich nach Bedarf. — Reimar Oltmanns zeigt die Entwicklung und Verstrickung einer leibhaftigen Romanfigur. Name: Jürgen W. Möllemann, Staatsminister. **16,80 DM** (1120)

Balzac könnte ihn erfunden haben, den Intriganten, den uns Reimar Oltmanns vorführt. Der Wandel vom Idealisten zum Machtfetischisten, der wie ein Asket lebt und geliebt werden möchte, ist faszinierend nachgezeichnet. Der Politik-Sucht-Kranke heißt Heiner Geißler, Generalsekretär der CDU. **16,80 DM** (1121)

Viele verabscheuen den »American way of life« und erliegen ihm doch. Warum? Weil die USA einer Droge gleichen. STERN-Amerika-Experte Liedtke pustet Vorurteile aus dem Schädel und zwingt Aha-Erlebnisse rein. Mit Fotos nur **20,— DM** (1028)

Walter Widmer: »Der entsetzlichste, erschütterndste Protest, der je gegen den Krieg erhoben wurde.« Wir fördern Johnny mit allem Nachdruck, weil es »das radikalste Anti-Kriegs-Buch ist, das je geschrieben wurde« — Ivan Illich. **Nur 18,— DM** (0112)

Ein einzigartiges Buch: liebenswert erzählte Tante-Lina-Geschichten, Dokumente aus der Kriegszeit und Kochrezepte von damals. Die Rheinische Post: »Tante Linas Kapriolen verraten Mut und Menschlichkeit, weniger den einer stillen Heldin, sondern mehr den einer Lebenskünstlerin mit Rückgrat.« **28,— DM** (1015)

Die »Trümmerfrauen«, die nach dem 2. Weltkrieg die Karre aus dem Dreck zogen, wie haben sie gelebt, was haben sie gedacht und vor allem: wie haben sie gekocht? — Zeitgeschichte für Kopf und Bauch. Mit vielen Rezepten, Geschichten und Dokumenten. **28,— DM** (1037)